Strong W.O.M.A.N. The Companion Journal

Strong W.O.M.A.N. The Companion Journal

Dr. Cheryl Edwards Buckingham, PhD

Thus Said Productions LLC

Journaling

Congrats on taking the next steps in becoming a Stronger Woman! There are many benefits to journaling. Journaling helps you to think about your thinking and can therefore assist you in continuing to develop into your best self. There are also health benefits that have been associated with journaling (aka expressive writing). The health benefits include improving immune functions, keeping your memory sharp, boosting your mood, and aiding with emotional functions (ex. regulating emotions, building self-confidence, boosting creativity and critical thinking). My prayer is that in using this journal and the journaling process, you will not only grow spiritually and become a Stronger Woman, but you will also reap the health benefits associated with journaling.

Some best practice tips to help you with journaling are to find the right space and setting to journal, set aside enough time to journal, don't rush yourself, don't procrastinate, and re-read your journaling to add additional thoughts for continued growth. Let's get started...

W–Wisdom

- What are your thoughts on Wisdom?
- How can you apply Wisdom to your everyday tasks? Create a Wisdom goal for yourself.
- Write out your steps and progress towards the goal.
- Once you have completed that goal, create another and repeat.

_____
_____
_____
_____
_____
_____
_____
_____
_____
_____
_____
_____
_____
_____
_____
_____
_____
_____

_____
_____
_____
_____
_____
_____
_____
_____
_____
_____
_____
_____
_____
_____
_____
_____
_____
_____
_____
_____
_____
_____
_____
_____
_____
_____
_____
_____
_____
_____
_____
_____
_____
_____

O-Overcomer

- Think about situations that you have overcame or that you have to overcome. What steps did you take to overcome?
- What steps can you take to overcome? How can you build on those steps for the future?

  Some of the steps I used were (1) Recognized that challenging situations were not too hard for God; (2) Took charge of my thoughts by finding scriptures that pertained to my specific situation, so that I could speak life into the situation; (3) Watched what I physically spoke and what others spoke about the situation (no negativity) (4) Made sure that I had on my spiritual armor (Ephesians 6:11-18); (5) Continued to pray and praise.

- Do you think these steps can help you? Write about it. Write out the challenge, the scriptures that pertain to overcoming it, positive words that you can speak over the challenge, how the spiritual armor can help you, and a prayer that you can repeat.

_____

_____

_____

_____

_____

_____

_____

_____

_____

_____
_____
_____
_____
_____
_____
_____
_____
_____
_____
_____
_____
_____
_____
_____
_____
_____
_____
_____
_____
_____
_____
_____
_____
_____
_____
_____
_____
_____
_____
_____
_____
_____

M-Modesty

- What are your thoughts on Modesty?
- Do you think Modesty is relevant and applicable in today's society? Why or why not?
- If you have not been applying Modesty, write some of the benefits that you can gain from Modesty.
- If you have been applying Modesty, write down how you think it has helped you.

_____

_____

_____

_____

_____

_____

_____

_____

_____

_____

_____

_____

_____

_____

_____

_____

A-Anointing

- What are your thoughts on the Anointing and the Holy Spirit? Do you believe in the trinity (Father God, Son Jesus, Holy Spirit)?
- Has there been a time in your life where you feel like the Anointing was present and/or the Holy Spirit intervened in a situation? Write about it... What happened and what were your emotions and reactions in the situation?
- If there has not been a time, think about and write about ways that you can allow the Anointing to flow (ex. quiet time).

_____
_____
_____
_____
_____
_____
_____
_____
_____
_____
_____
_____
_____
_____
_____

N- Nurturer

- What are your thoughts on being a Nurturer?
- Have you ever guided, trained, supported, took care of, or encouraged someone?
- If yes, write about how the situation made you feel. If it was positive, think about and write about how you can increase and expand on nurturing in the future. If the experience was negative, write about what could have happened to turn it into a positive, and use this as a development tool for the future.
- If no, think about and write about how you can personally develop and become a Nurturer and then practice it (ex. finding, reading and writing Bible scriptures on love and showing/practicing love).

_____
_____
_____
_____
_____
_____
_____
_____
_____
_____
_____
_____

_____

_____

_____

_____

_____

_____

_____

_____

_____

_____

_____

_____

_____

_____

_____

_____

_____

_____

_____

_____

_____

_____

_____

_____

_____

_____

_____

_____

_____

_____

_____

www.ingramcontent.com/pod-product-compliance
Lightning Source LLC
Chambersburg PA
CBHW051455290426
44109CB00016B/1759